All in the Family

Dona Herweck Rice

I0883337

Consultants

Sally Creel, Ed.D.
Curriculum Consultant

Leann Iacuone, M.A.T., NBCT, ATC
Riverside Unified School District

Jill Tobin
California Teacher of the Year
Semi-Finalist
Burbank Unified School District

Image Credits: p.11 Corbis/age fotostock; pp.20–21 (illustrations) Chris Sabatino; all other images from Shutterstock.

Library of Congress Cataloging-in-Publication Data

Rice, Dona, author.
All in the family / Dona Herweck Rice; consultants, Sally Creel, Ed.D. curriculum consultant, Leann Iacuone, M.A.T., NBCT, ATC Riverside Unified School District, Jill Tobin, California Teacher of the Year Semi-Finalist, Burbank Unified School District.
pages cm
Summary: "Have you ever noticed that offspring look like their parents? That is because they have the same genes. Genes make you who you are. But you will always be unique!"— Provided by publisher.
Audience: Grades K to 3.
Includes index.
ISBN 978-1-4807-4563-6 (paperbook)
ISBN 978-1-4807-5053-1 (ebook)
1. Genetics—Juvenile literature.
2. Heredity—Juvenile literature. I. Title.
QH437.5.R53 2015
576.5—dc23

2014013148

Teacher Created Materials
5301 Oceanus Drive
Huntington Beach, CA 92649-1030
http://www.tcmpub.com

ISBN 978-1-4807-4563-6
© 2015 Teacher Created Materials, Inc.

Printed by: 584728
Printed In: India
PO#: 16147

Table of Contents

We Go Together

Who is the parent and who is the baby? It is easy to tell. You can just look to see that some things go together.

This is a mother bear with her cub.

This young plant will grow up to be a large tree.

Living things that go together belong to the same **species** (SPEE-seez). They are a lot like other members of the species. They look, sound, move, and act in **similar** ways.

Close but Not Exact

Members of a species are not exactly alike. But they are very close.

These flowers are all roses. But they do not look exactly the same.

These are all orangutans (aw-RANG-oo-tanz). They are similar.

Traits

Members of the same species have common **traits**. A trait shows what something is by how it looks or acts.

Palm trees have traits to help them grow in the sand.

Each living thing gets its traits from its parents. Human parents pass their traits to their kids. Animals and plants pass their traits, too.

Birds of a Feather

These birds have white feathers. Their parents have white feathers, too.

Our bodies know what traits we have. We are born with our traits. Animals and plants are also born with their traits.

This scientist studies traits.

This pup will hunt just like its mother does. That is its trait.

For example, think about the traits in two frogs of the same species. They are similar. One frog might have a trait to be greener. One frog might have a trait to be smaller. But the frogs are mainly the same!

These frogs have different traits.

Frog Species

There are about 5,000 frog species in the world!

Traits tell how a thing looks. They make a plant grow flowers. They make a dog have spots. Or they make a person have curly hair.

This plant grows flowers because of its traits.

This dog has traits for spots.

This boy has traits for curly hair.

Traits also tell how a thing acts. Traits make a flower open in the sun. They make a puppy want to run and play. And they make a person want to learn about the world.

This boy's traits make him want to learn.

This puppy plays because of its traits.

This flower opens because of its traits.

Unique

Each member of a species is alike. But it is also **unique** (yoo-NEEK). It is not the same as anything else.

That is true for you. It is true for all living things. Each thing is a lot like its parents. But it is the only thing exactly like itself!

Each living thing is unique.

Let's Do Science!

Are animal and plant babies exactly like their parents? Try this and see!

What to Get

- lima beans or other fast-growing seeds
- paper and pencil
- potting soil and containers
- water

What to Do

1. Plant some lima bean seeds in soil. Water them. Put them in the sun.

2. Watch the plant grow. Draw a picture of it every few days. On each picture, write how old the plant is.

3. When it sprouts new seeds, plant them. Take care of the new plant. Draw pictures of it, too. Write how old both plants are.

4. Compare the plants and their pictures after a few days. How are the plants alike? How are they different?

Glossary

similar—alike or close to the same

species—a group of related plants or animals that look like each other and have similar traits

traits—things that tell how something looks or behaves

unique—unlike anything else

Index

Your Turn!

Plant Traits

All living things have traits. Look at some plants around you. In what ways are they like other plants? In what ways are they unique? Draw the different plant traits that you see.